Is That What They Told You?

Selected Poems

Is That What They Told You?

Selected Poems

Peter K. Schotch

ISBN 978-0-9780552-3-3

Contents

Chapter 1

Introduction

When one is confronted by a *selection* of something or other, questions naturally arise. Selected by whom? What was the criterion which guided the selection? After the selection was made, how many were left out. And so on until, to quote Charles Pierce, at last we are glad to sleep in death.

I shall do my best to answer some of these questions. I was the selector. I read through all my accumulated poetry—about 25 years worth, and ordered them by their cringe-quotient. I then picked the ones with the smallest. Well, sort of. There are still some cringey ones, but others have liked them, so they snuck in by the side-door. I have also omitted any of my longer poems; some because they weren't quite ready for publication, and others because they never will be.

Chapter 2

Philosophers Without Bladders

Cogito

I exist. I intend to keep on existing,
until I run out of
shoes

The Consolation of Philosophy

Do you love wisdom more than life?
Or do you squirm a bit
and writhe with envy in your gut
when confronted by the wise?

Do you say in your inmost heart:
"How I long to be that wise!"?
Or do you say instead: "If she's so smart,
how come he isn't rich?"?

But only think, if you were wise
then you'd have that, no matter
into which wallow of festering folly
you fell.

Mind you, that folly'd stick some.
And then there's these sundry folk
who'd flee you
and your corrosive sagacity.

Don't want any on 'em, see?
But most of all the thing they do not want
is knowing.
Because once you know—that's it.

Actual Transcription - Donuts

Me: I'll have a dozen donuts please.
She: Do you want them all the same?

Me: If they were all the same there'd only be one.
She: Next!

Actual Transcription - Famous Quotes

He: Hello and thanks for calling.
Me: You're welcome; I'm calling from the university

He: About...?
Me: I was looking through the yellow pages and came across your ad.
He: Oh yes?
Me: It was your use of quotation that caught my eye.
He: Quotation?

Me: Just so. At the top of your ad you have "service" is our motto.
He: So ...?

Me: As an expert on quotation, I can tell you that the standard parsing of that, implies that what you mean by service is not what people ordinarily mean.
He: Are you sure about that; it sounds kind of goofy to me.

Me: Trust me on this, the way you have things, that use of quotation would most readily be interpreted as scare quotes.

He: Scarecrows? That really is goofy.

Me: No no. Scare *quotes*. As in he told me a " funny" story. If you were to read that you would take it to mean that the story was not funny. See?
He: (with a sigh) Okay; yeah; I can sort of see that. What should the ad say instead?

Me: Hmmm, that's a bit tricky but the best thing would be "service is our motto" is our motto.
He: click

Actual Transcription—Truth(1)

He: There is no truth!
Me: Not even that?

He: Huh?

Actual Transcription—Truth(2)

She: Is what you said true?
He: Isn't that all relative?

She: Certainly not!
He: Ah, but that is only true for you!

She: Not only is it true for me, but it is also true for
      me that it is true for you.
He: huh?

Actual Transcription—Epistemology

He: I don't know the answer.
She: Have you even *tried* knowing?

He: Huh?

The Cathedral of Unlearning

Do you know what
knowledge is?
Could you know that
you don't?

If you were in pain,
would you know it?
How about if I were in
pain,
would you know that?

I didn't think so.

The Problem of the External World

When you get right down to it,
what we call 'the world' is just
a bunch of signals,
and we so many receivers.
How's your
bandwidth, baby?

"Surely" you say,
"If there are signals,
then something is signaling,
something noumenal."

Alas, common sense
falls to the ground
again.
After all, light is a wave
but what is waving?
And don't call me "Shirley"!

Personal Identity

There is a question
we must answer.
It's not:
"Why must I do these things?"
though that is what
you often ask.
The question is:
"If I weren't doing
in this way,
would it really be me,
that person who is
not doing it?"

[hint] The usual answer is
"That depends."

Virtu

Did we all do what we should
And not what we would rather
Would we bring about the Good,
Or any of that blather?

If you did just what you ought
Instead of what you want,
You'd have what you'd rather not
And nothing much to flaunt.

"Virtue is its own reward"
Is what they often mutter
Who never have been truly bored
Nor felt their hearts once flutter.

Veritas Vincit

Take all the lies
You tell every day
Bind them together
And call it a play.

Cast into stone
Or just cream of wheat,
Truth can be sour
And lies can be sweet.

Always remember:
The truth you now tell
That seems so compelling,
Tomorrow will smell.

Felix Conjunctio

I'll run to the store and
buy us some fresh thyme.

I'd really like to hear your explanation
of why you went and
did that.

You should try and
remember what we are doing here.

Just do your job and
stop wasting time.

Do as I say and
not as I do.

Chapter 3

Autobiography

Another Story Of My Life

So I asked her if she'd like to do some
phone sex
And she said:
"Not tonight dear,
I have an
earache."

All Hallows Eve

Sometimes I feel like
Frankenstein
And you certainly make a plausible
Igor.

Unreal Estate

People often tell me that
I spend too much time
living in my head,
but they are mistaken.

I tried living in my head once,
but my mind was
closed.

I like to think of myself
as a man of the world,
but not this
world.

Sometimes you settle

I've finally selected
my workout
tape:
Six weeks to
buns of lead.

Dialing It Back a Bit

Live each day as if
it were your
ante-penultimate

The Humor of our Time

Do I have to;
Must I;
Am I compelled to
make a joke of everything?
Is what you want to know.

So serious you are
and hurt and angry
With it.
But when you're so serious
you have a way of making
your face smaller
with the seriousness of it all
And noticing that, I am nearly
Wrecked again
On the reefs and shoals
Of your frown.

I am a man driven
before the gales of laughter
Which blow at these latitudes.
But that makes me more of a
Flying Dutchman than a
Laughing Cavalier,
wouldn't you say?

I'm sure it must be hard,
but I want you finally to consider:
If we never make light,
we shall make only
Darkness.

Life begins at aleph-null

Some days I feel like the
wreck of the Phosphorus
and others like the
statue of Limitations.

But even the energetic
must find it harder and
harder
to be the hero
of the story
of their lives.

You take the other day
for instance.

"Save me from myself!"
she cried, as she threw
herself in the general direction
of my ankles.
"I'd rather save you from
me" I allowed with
becoming honesty.

That's a Miss

I fired one of my
metaphors
into the literary
air.
It fell to earth
with a very dull
thud,
right there.
Right where everybody
could see it.

I know:
Don't quit my day job,
right?

On Being the Right Size

Art holds holds a
mirror up to Life.
We often forget though:
Objects in the mirror
are closer than they
appear to be.

For sure my life is
way too close
for comfort.

Cosmetic Flaw

I have no regrets
but I do have
too much
eyebrow.

They bristle at the
world
and cause the
Meek
to think me
Fierce
And the Fierce to
think me an
opportunist.

No But Honestly...

O let's undo the little fibs
Which clothe the two of us.
So we can count each other's ribs
And make a pretty fuss.

"It's not so bad," will be our cry
"To see you in your skin."
And if you aren't so very spry
Then neither am I thin.

"Is that your real libido, dear?
I thought it would be grander!"
Your smile so full of lovely cheer,
I almost like your candor.

Talking To You Is Like Talking To A Brick Wall

What you need to do is,
buckle down!
Work doesn't do itself, you know.
I like fun too, as much as the
next person, but
does it pay the bills?

I'll tell you what your
problem is:
You don't look for
things to do.

There are all these rat-holes.
Look!
You could be pounding sand down them
right now.
but instead you
scribble.

Comments and Criticism I

And when I finished
reading,
she smiled into the
middle distance,
the kind of
forced smile people wear
when their dog
farts at a cocktail party.

"That's very nice,
Dear."
she murmured uncertainly.

Angst

Hey!
My life is no bed of roses,
you know.
Well, I suppose that maybe
it actually is.

I did have that
flat tire
A while back and my
dishwasher is broken.
That has to count for
something.

Listen!
I do my best to keep myself
filled with rage
and despair,
but I
leak.

The Truth About Sisyphus

We do what we can
and not what we will.
Sometimes,
we don't manage even
that much.
I mean
what with this damp
weather
and all.

Synchronicity

what an amazing
coincidence
that you should be
thinking of me
at the exact same time
that I was
too.

Vision Quest

How I love to be
the apple
of your eye.
Thy rods and thy cones,
they comfort me.

Quick Off The Mark

I've lived a dozen
lifetimes
while you were waiting
for permission
to start
living.

Of course I haven't
actually
done
anything much.

Heroes of Antique Mien

Hector of
the flashing helm,
tries so hard to
overwhelm.

Would it kill you
to take a day
off
now and then?

Achilles, sulking
in his tent,
never had to
pay the rent.
Anybody can sulk
in a tent.
I can sulk in a
split-level
three-bedroom
house.

Youropia Too

Yes I do have a pair
of glasses,
but I only need them
for
seeing.

And I Coveted Her Ass, Too

Wanting is a
gift.
If you wanted
nothing,
you'd be dead.

I knew this girl once;
she could really want.
You name it, she'd
want it.
She could want a hole
in a cast-iron
bucket.

The only thing she
didn't want
was me.
I was crushed.

Through A Glass Darkly

My father, if the truth be told,
had many flaws (let's call them).
When I was young, I promised bold
that I would not be like him.

Now that I am older though,
it's very plain to see:
that even though I'm not like him,
still he was quite like me.

Senior Moments

Years of gold.
Ears of lead.

Should I wonder what you said?
Would it matter if I did?

Do I dare to do that thing.
You know what I mean.

That thing with the thing.

Chapter 4

Les Pèchès

Are you talking to me?

Anger is a white-hot flame
which cleanses us when needful,
Of all the wretched fear and shame
To which we are so heedful.

It burns away those niggling doubts
that stop our furious venture.
It deafens us to reason's shouts,
and turns away from censure.

The thing is:
Sometimes you just
get really
pissed off,
you know?

Another deadly sin

I spend hours at the gym
every goddam day.
I have to, or else
I bloat up like
wonder pig.

I never touch
alcohol.
The only thing I ever
drink
is this bottled water from
Greenland.

Meat?
Have you any idea
at all,
what that stuff
does to you?

It's important to look
after yourself.
And just because my
haircut cost a hundred dollars or so, doesn't
make me a bad person.
Does it?

Envy

I suffered from a
nameless dread,
along about last week.
And on that day
I cursed the bread
devoured by the meek.

Let their ships
all suffer wreck.
Let them dine on stones.
Let there be a disconnect
afflicting all their phones.

I mean,
these bozos are going to
inherit the earth,
right?

Lust

The arc of my desire
Has welded me to you.
My loins are made of fire
And yours are made of glue.

The engine of your yearning
has driven you to me.
Your eyes are large and burning,
While mine have shrunk with glee.

The grip of heated passion
admits of no escape.
So let us start a fashion
and hide behind no drape.

Chapter 5

The World

Comments and Criticism II

It fell off the tongue
in a ponderous beautiful
rush,
that poem.
Like spitting out a mouthful of
graceful ball bearings.

As we picked ourselves up off
the floor of our minds,
we all looked at her
and said
"kewl!"

Career Counseling

If you want money,
go for the money.
There are people who
will despise
you
for it,
but they're probably just
envious.

And let's face it:
There will always be
people who despise
you.
There were people who
despised Albert
Fucking
Schweitzer.

And It's Not Discrete

An attempt at plucky valor
mostly finds the lesser
part, which is
spleen.

Career Counseling II

If you want respect,
go for the money.
That's the world we
live in.

If, on the other hand,
you want your name
to be remembered for
hundreds of years,
then
be the first
to set yourself on fire
in the middle of
the Republican National
Convention.

And many happy returns

So you're back again,
are you?
Yet another case of
deja vous.

Mythic Ponderings

Come wonder at the Phoenix,
so regal and so dire!
Do you suppose his penix
is also made of fire?

Three Ages of Person

I am young.
I can do whatever I want
because of that.
The world prizes
my youth.
The thing is:
How do you figure out what you want?

I am old.
I can do whatever I want
because of my gray hairs
and my experience
and I'm going to die soon anyway
so fuck you.
The thing is:
There really isn't anything
that I want.

I am neither young nor
am I elderly.
I have a fair amount of past but not
all of it, not yet.
I don't know if I can do what
I want, or not.
I only know that I'm sick
to death
of doing
this.

Domestic Arrangements

You bring me tea.
I bring you a litany of
fresh disasters.

Austere Interiors

A bird, I've heard, has hollow bones
the better for to fly.
I make do with hollow moans
and shun the empty sky.
And what of you, my bosom friend?
Do you contain a vacuum too;
a sudden coming to an end
of the journey into you?
Well, I wouldn't worry about it
if I were you.
After all, you know what they say:
Voids will be voids.

Just another talk-show host

It fits me like a second skin,
My sense of indignation.
And even though I seldom win,
It keeps me at my station.

The mighty always hear me stomp
As to their place I travel,
To hector them about their pomp,
My voice like red-hot gravel.
"And what have you done recently"
I shout as sounding brasses
"To justify your making free
With all your neighbors" asses?"

Epistle to the Effusions (Draft)

What shall it profit a man
if he gains the whole
world,
but has
bad breath?

Mind you,
if somebody gained
the whole world,
WeightWatchers(tm) should
probably be informed.

Breakfast of Also Rans

On the bagel of my life
You are the loxsmith
at which Love laughs.

Close, But No Cigar

My master plan for
world peace
was entirely undermined
when they noticed those
unsightly flakes of
dandruff.

Civilization

I read the
Classic Comic
of
War and Peace
today.

That Tolstoy guy,
he can
really draw!

But Not Out Of Mind

And have you fallen then
through a crack in the Absolute, perhaps?
Well, it's just as
I have always said
about
fallen
women.

Every Day, In Every Way ...

I have a new
mantram
these days.
It goes:

Maybe
it won't be
as bad
as I
think.

There's a lot to be
said for the
power of
positive thinking.

Notes From Your Life-Coach

Be mindful!
Live in the moment!
No, not *that*
moment,
this one over here!

Remember that the destination
doesn't matter compared to the
journey!

So basically, getting there
is all the
fun.

Spur of the Torment

Give me a reason,
I'll give you a rhyme
Give me a place
And I'll make the time
To run up your stairs;
To knock on your door
So but me no buts
Lest I stick in my or.

Lust Among the Rushes

You don't need power
to love.
what you need is
ignorance and
knowledge,
all at once.

Unless of course
we are talking about
love in the
fast lane.

In which case
-wham-
what you need
-bam-
is a short
-thank you!-
memory

Paradoxes of the Newly Virtuous

How curious that you
cannot abide
smoke,
whose whole life is
mirrors.

Visual Aid

If you took the people who
didn't fancy me at all and
put them end-to-end,
the line would
stretch
from here to
there.

In fact,
why not try it?

I'd Rather Be Saline

My tears
could kill a pod of
sad snails
before they dart their lust.
But then,
I'm an old
salt.

Mental Health

People often ask me how
I keep myself so clean.
And I reply, with genteel bow,
By venting all my spleen.

You could be immaculate
In similar degree.
All you have to do is let
Your bile and rage spill free.

Never call a spade "a spade"
Or cower in your hovel,
Show the steel of which you're made
And say: "A fucking shovel!"

Feeding Frenzy

Many and
various are the
teeth of my
thinking.

I bite off
small chunks of your
mind;
I smack my thin but sensuous
lips:

Al dente!

And Not Just Oaks!

If you're down, just
give a thought to this:
The mighty Achilles
was once but
Thetis'
fetus.

Emotional Self-defence

You say that
If I really loved you,
I'd let you
strangle me.

How about if I just
hold my breath for a
Really long time?

ASAP Fable

Somebody stole her
necklace, and
She wept,
until she met a
woman who had no
neck.

Supermodel

She smiled once,
in sad defiance of
her
cheekbones.

It Augers Well

I read the
future in your sweaty
palm
and in the leavings of your
T-Shirt.

You will soon meet a
stranger of medium height,
and thinning hair,
Who could stand to miss a few
Meals.

Uncanny, isn't it?

Watching My Six

I can't help thinking,
seeing you like this,
that you have the look
of a deer caught in the
tail-lights.

We Gave At The Office

There came a knocking at my door.
One knock.
Two.
A dozen.
A score.

So I could tell right off that
it wasn't
Opportunity.

Romantic Interlude

I wined her.
I dined her.
I waltzed her out the
French doors and onto the
terrace.

As we looked out over the
Adriatic and the moonlight
glinted softly on my
patent leather shoes,
I crushed her to my
manly bosom and asked her to be mine
forever.

She smiled shyly.
The breeze wafted some
hair across her face in
a dark cloud of
unknowing, and she
told me with a toss of her shapely
head,

that she didn't think it would be
appropriate
at this time.

Polite Forms

He went
to the bathroom
in his pants,
you say?

Well,
it's a damn good thing,
isn't it,
that he had that little bathroom
with him.
Otherwise,
he'd have pissed himself
for sure.

Paragon

Her hair was like
a living thing;
it flowed from here
to there.
And everywhere
that Mary went
there followed close her
hair.

Her eyes were like
two limpid pools,
so soft and also
wise.
And when she had
a cross to bear,
she always crossed her
eyes.

Triptych

Yeah but ...

Salamanders, so I'm told,
All have a special grace.
A sinuosity so bold,
It's always in your face.

Our fumblings on the other hand,
Are rarely so refined.
We seldom rise above the bland
And often lead the blind.

But even if it's they not we
Who are so very scenic,
We can at least their rivals be
At being unhygienic.

Slippery too ...

Salad mongers?
well there was that grocer
across the street,
but he didn't start any
fires.
At least, nothing was ever
proved.

But with a special grace

Salamanca?
Yes, we were there last year.
I'll say they are graceful!
There was this one chap
at our hotel
who could tie his shoelaces
together
and then take off his
trousers.

Optimism

Some people fear that age will
take from them
all that they find dear,
stripping them a bit each day
of that which makes them wonderful.

But you're getting better
every day in every way.
At the end, when you die,
you're perfect.

Our flaws are leaches on us,
feeding on our youth.
They drop from us when they can batten no longer.
And we glow, ever more heated.
until the earth can no longer contain
our blazing perfection, don't you see?

Vivat!

When I consider suicide
It seems the very neatest scheme,
Until I realize that 'died'
Would be my one and only meme.

For while the dead don't track in dirt
Or suffer daily from bad knees,
Neither do they ever flirt
Nor stand around and shoot the breeze.

So I'll continue with my list:
"Go get laid" and "read the paper",
Not assuming I'll be missed
Once I meet that old Grim Raper.

We've Been In The Wars

The war on drugs:
Drugs won.

The war on terror:
Nobody won.
They ran out of terror, and we ran out of war.

The war on poverty:
Rich people won.

The war on prepositions:
We got bored of it after a couple months.

The war on Christmas:
Called on account of stupid.

Well?

If brevity be the soul of wit:

How To Excel at Sports

Practice the basic fundamentals.
Don't let yourself vacillate back and forth.

If you follow this advice, you will have
good success.